Endorsements

In a world where women are expected to be perfectly polished wives, mothers, and career-makers, rarely do we ever push pause on these expectations and walk in the truth of what God has called us to be. This book is a story of redemption that encourages women to see a clear picture of what freedom through Christ truly is.

– Anonymous

Forgiven Sinner is beautifully bold in how she shares her heart, past, and most intimate moments. As a body of believers I think we would all be more free to live fully alive and filled with joy if we shared our vulnerable realities in life with our sacred community of friends, seeking God's goodness in the midst of our messy. I pray this book helps you share openly with a trusted friend the beautiful story God is writing in your life.

– Elizabeth Hochart, Noonday Ambassador

Life can be cruel and just plain hard. We can go through times of feeling like we don't add up, unfit to be loved, failing as a spouse or a parent and wondering what the "American dream" really means. Forgiven Sinner's story of overcoming not just obstacles in marriage and parenting but also making decisions on chasing that move up the corporate ladder can seem all too familiar to a lot of us. Her choice to lean solely on Jesus to give her purpose and true fulfillment in life should be freeing for anyone who reads "Unexplainable Freedom."

— **Jeremy Affeldt**, Retired MLB Pitcher
3x World Series Champion

Unexplainable Freedom

by Forgiven Sinner

WESTBOW
PRESS®
A DIVISION OF THOMAS NELSON
& ZONDERVAN

WestBow Press books may be ordered through booksellers or by contacting:

WestBow Press
A Division of Thomas Nelson & Zondervan
1663 Liberty Drive
Bloomington, IN 47403
www.westbowpress.com
1 (866) 928-1240

ISBN: 978-1-9736-4807-9 (sc)
ISBN: 978-1-9736-4808-6 (hc)
ISBN: 978-1-9736-4806-2 (e)

Library of Congress Control Number: 2018914574

Print information available on the last page.

WestBow Press rev. date: 02/21/2019

Acknowledgements

To my husband, my best friend, thank you for choosing me to do life with. For loving me unconditionally and encouraging me to pursue the callings God puts on my heart. You believe in me and challenge me in ways that make me better. You are the best dad I could have ever asked for and I am so very grateful for the ways you make us all laugh and most importantly the ways you teach us to love others well.

To my children, you have no idea how proud I am of each of you. You are my pride and joy. I love getting to share life with you and be a part of pointing you to the truth of how much God loves you. Please forgive me for the numerous times I have and will fail you. Remember who you are fathered by and never doubt the love he has for you. Be in relationship with Jesus every single day. He will never fail you. Go be servant hearted, loving and kind, and proud of the faith you have chosen.

To my cousin for helping make this book a reality, my sister-in-law for editing, my immediate family for encouraging, and for so many friends and extended family who have believed in me along the way. Thank you!

To my Abba Father, I love you. Thank you for loving me so, so well!

From,

Forgiven Sinner

To learn more about Forgiven Sinner or if you would like to contact her visit www.savvymommas.org.

Intro: All For God's Glory

I have dreamt of publishing a book for many years. One that would inspire other people; keep me excited to want to keep coming back to my computer to work; and one that gives great hope to people who might have a similar story. I envisioned writing children's stories, self-help books, and devotionals. It never occurred to me to simply tell the story of my life. But that was the calling that ended up staring me right in the face. I would ask myself, "Who would even care to pick up a book and read about my life? No one really knows me. My life doesn't really matter to other people!"

Then I realized, writing this book isn't about me. It's about the real author who created me. I am just one of the characters in a story. The author who has written every detail deserves the credit. I just get to be the character that comes to share the story of redemption, pursuit, desire, and forgiveness with anyone that is looking for deeper answers. It is his story, and I just get to be a part of his work.

In case you do not know about this author, let me be the first to tell you that he is writing a story in you, too. My questions are these: Are you allowing him to be the author? Have you given him full reign to decide what will happen next? How will you move forward, and when will you be able to reveal the greatest discovery of your life is Jesus Christ? The story in each of our lives never ends until he calls us home. How will you live out the story that he has for you? Will you be a doer of his vision for your life? Or will you do what you want, on your time, and with your people? Will the desires he has for your life be fulfilled when you pursue him and carry out his story?

I am about to unveil the good, the bad, and the ugly of the story Jesus has written and is still writing on my own life. An ordinary girl, in an ordinary world. Yet somehow Jesus came alive in my soul and took me from being ordinary to living an extraordinary life on a mission for loving others. A mission that has set my heart on fire and awakened my inner being to live with purpose, fulfillment, gratitude, and great joy. Will you join me on this mission of unlocking the key to your own story?

Chapter 1

The Early Years

My childhood began like many other upper-middle-class suburban Americans. I grew up in Texas in the same house from the age of two until I was eighteen and went to college. My mom, dad, brother, sister, and I lived in a small, predominately white town with an average to above-average lifestyle. I had my own room, a pool in the backyard, neighbors to play with, a country club to swim at, a church to call home, and friends whose lives were similar to mine. As a child, I have fond memories with my family. From vacations to Colorado, Canada, Florida, and California to countless family gatherings with cousins, aunts, uncles, and grandparents. We celebrated the holidays traditionally with our extended family and immersed our lives in our local school and church community. We attended Friday night football, went Christmas caroling from the back of a trailer filled with bales of hay, participated in school plays, ran in Saturday morning track meets, grilled steaks on the weekends, and spent plenty of time devoted to our church. At church there was Sunday school, choir, drama team, and Wednesday night dinners.

My family spent a lot of time at our Baptist church. Of course, that meant a strict set of rules like no slumber parties on Saturday nights unless I promised to be at church on Sundays. Church was just a part of life as far as I was concerned. I did not really know anything different. There are parts about the routine that gave me a sense of security, helped build a foundation for biblical teachings, and allowed me the chance to see what Christian community can look like.

Ironically, this outwardly pious and seemingly "right" way of living had very little to do with having a relationship with Jesus Christ. It was simply a lifestyle. A routine. A religion. And it certainly consumed an aspect of my identity, although looking back, I don't think it was what God had in mind. I made sure all my friends knew I was a Christian. I wore that boastful badge like a consummate Goody Two-shoes. I am pretty sure I went to the altar at least four times to rededicate my life to Christ. It never hurts to make sure, right? I know good and well Jesus was pursuing me. And I did a fairly good job of seeking him out, when I felt like I needed him.

But I would quickly fall off the bandwagon when things were going well in my life. The truth is I didn't need God to help because I thought I was doing pretty well on my own. It never connected for me—at least not until much later in life—that choosing a life with Jesus is something I must actively choose to do every single day.

I wish I knew then what I know now. (Don't we all?) But that isn't how God wrote this story. He knew he would need to break me. He knew life experiences were going to have to rattle me for him to become my all in all.

My brother is six years older than me. In my eyes, he was the golden child. Something about him could do no wrong. He was handsome, athletic, popular, smart, and the pride and joy of my dad's life. I never saw him make a mistake. I never saw him get into trouble. He was successful at all that he took part in, and my dad worshipped the ground he walked on. There was a shrine of my brother's football career in the game room. I am talking an entire room dedicated to just him. It had pictures of him running, jumping, and catching, as well as winning awards and wearing his uniform. All were performance-based pictures that my dad hung his hat on. I was always so proud of my brother. I loved bragging about him, inviting friends over on the weekend to watch his games on TV, and scheduling our entire weekends around his sports. He had the most amazing group of guy friends who always made my sister and me feel so special. They would make us laugh and treat us like their own sisters. And despite his glorified position in the family, he was humble, funny, and easy to be around. I appreciate this so much. Today, he is one of my best friends.

My sister is three years older than me and has a stronger opinion and personality than anyone I know—not in a bad way either. Let me be the first to tell you that you want my sister on your side. She will be your biggest fan, loudest cheerleader, and proudest friend you will ever have. But if you get on her bad side, you may want to run to China because she will be the first to put you in your place.

My sister was not athletic while growing up. Sports did not come easy for her. Neither did school. She had to work very hard for her grades and always tried to be a part of the sports teams. She is the one who would climb the soccer goal and get her entire body tangled in the net as the goalie for the neighborhood team. You could see her picking daisies in the field or just plain goofing off on the basketball court while trying to make the best of her situation. My goodness, this girl was funny! She could make anyone laugh—and she hasn't changed a bit to this day. She knew she was not the best athlete or student, but she still tried to find her way in our family in an effort to connect with my dad. Her siblings were stiff competition for her, but she managed to be one of the strongest and most resilient out of all of us. Funny how God works, isn't it?

Sadly, it was clear to all of us that my dad did not value her as much as he did my brother or me. He only knew how to love someone based on performance and perfection. She was an enigma to him. While she did not take the route of sports or academics, she had something else going for her. She was tall, beautiful, and full of life. In high school, she began modeling with a local agency. It gave her a confidence I had never seen in her before. I think that may have been the first time my dad showed much interest in what she was doing. He just did not know how to connect unless we were doing something that would make him proud.

I am the baby of the family. Being the baby meant my parents probably let me get away with a little bit more than my siblings did. It also meant I learned early to put a lot of pressure on myself to gain approval from my dad. I knew I had to perform to be accepted and loved by him. That is why I worked so hard at being the best at everything I tried. I did not want to fail him. Sometimes, I would succeed. Other times, I would not. And if one of my siblings happened to be in the spotlight, it put that much more pressure on me to outdo their efforts—just to feel like he loved me too.

As a baby, I took on the role of having to be perfect at everything, and eventually that took a toll on me. I definitely felt that as long as I was doing well at things then my dad was pleased and even proud of me. But I was far from perfect, which meant there were a lot of times I did not feel the unconditional love that every girl longs for from her father. I imagine that is not an unusual place to be for a lot of girls. We live in a broken world, after all.

My mom was tender, caring, and hands-on. She always had meals prepared on time and the house in order. She helped with my homework, took me to my practices, and kept the home environment a peaceful place. I never remember hearing any fights between her and my dad. I also never remember her ever standing up for what she believed in or giving her two cents about issues in our home. Whatever my dad did or said was the last of it. I believe she had to walk on eggshells every day of her life to keep the peace and remain a family of five. She was determined to never end up in a divorce and would just push her feelings or thoughts under the rug to avoid any outbursts. She was the epitome of a submissive wife. The only problem with that was that she never had a voice of her own or felt any value around my dad.

I know now why my dad was the way he was. He was not perfect, but I do think he was doing the best he could. He showed his love for us the same way his parents showed him love as a kid. It was all he knew. My dad grew up in a well-to-do community where success and status mattered. He worked hard trying to keep that same standard of status in his own life with our family. He was a successful businessman during my early childhood years, but things took a turn for the worse when I entered high school. He lost his job. His son, whom he had poured all of his energy into, was finishing up his college football career. He was entering a midlife crisis, and his sense of confidence began to flounder. He had lost pride in himself, and the family image he had worked hard to paste together was beginning to depart from the confines of his control.

Like most girls, I experienced a lot of highs and lows throughout my adolescence. I was fortunate to be athletic enough to make the competitive sports teams at school, which kept me busy and gave me confidence. I managed to make a lot of friends, but developed a habit of not being kind or selfless enough to keep them around. I spent much more time trying to be perfect at everything. I felt a driving need to fit the mold my family had worked so hard to create.

I was the kind of typical American Christian teenager that pretended to be perfect and I was lethally judgmental towards others around me. The Bible was my rulebook and I did my best to appear as though I was following all the rules. I knew a lot of Bible stories and verses. I went to church camp in the summer and came back each time with a renewed sense of purpose for living the perfect Christian life. But inside, I was so frail. I was insecure; terrified of what people would think if they knew that I was just as empty and clueless as everyone I seemed so quick to judge. Despite my near flawless attempts to appear like I had it all together, I failed to recognize that the religion I was blindly following had a man named Jesus at the center of it who was so much more than a prophet, or part of a history book. I was blind to the truth about where to grasp my real source of strength: in him.

In high school, I liked to flirt with the possibility of being rebellious. But I would always end up back in my comfortable "Goodie Two-shoes." I would go to church on Sunday mornings, but sneak out to grab donuts a few blocks away with friends without my parents ever knowing. I started going to weekend parties—you know, the kind of thrown together keg socials hosted in a vacant field somewhere on the outskirts of town? There was plenty of beer and ample time to see-and-be-seen. But my bold attempt to be "cool," was always thwarted by my inner fear that my parents would be so ashamed of my presence there. I would inevitably call them and ask them to come pick me up. My guilty conscience was their pride and joy. They would always express how proud they were of me for doing the right thing. It never quite added up to them that I had made the decision to go there in the first place.

That nagging feeling deep inside that wanted me to recognize right from wrong? That was the Holy Spirit. He had long been a presence inside of me, but I had a knack for ignoring him, leaning just a little too far in the other direction. I would drink beer on occasion, blur the lines of promiscuity with boys, and sabotage friendships by ruthlessly insisting on an appearance of having it all together. Looking back, I was a lot more concerned about disappointing my parents than about disappointing my heavenly father. I became a master at appearing perfect. Cute clothes, lustrous hair, a winning attitude, and a lip-glossed smile to make sure nobody could doubt me. But inside I was like a caged rabbit, heart always pounding. I was constantly nervous, insecure, scared that someone might discover how unconfident, uncomfortable, and terrified of life I really was. I was a wreck.

1. *How did you see yourself as a child? Were you happy? Shy? Silly? Safe? Scared?*

2. *Do you find yourself living with regret from your past and maybe need to ask God for forgiveness for some of your poor choices?*

3. *What type of parenting approach did your parents take? What are some things they did that you loved and do today in your own family? What are some things they did that you hated and wanted to break the mold?*

4. *Where did you see God in your early years? Think back. Even if you never heard of him-are there places where he protected you? Inspired you? Brought you important relationships that really mattered or defined a lot of who you became?*

Chapter 2

Young Love and Heartbroken

I fell in love when I was 16 years old. It was with the "new guy" on campus that everyone was talking about. He was a perfect 10. Tall, dark, handsome, athletic, charming, and a friend to everyone he met. I remember all of the girls on my volleyball team talking about him as "the one" to pursue. I giggled along with them, and quietly wondered if he would ever give someone like me the time of day. At one of those weekend field parties one Saturday, I justified my attendance by recruiting anyone that would listen to come with me to a Christian summer camp in North Carolina through Young Life, a Christian youth ministry. Before I knew it, the "new guy" quickly chimed in about how awesome Young Life was and how he would totally go with me to camp. As he stood there, holding a can of light beer in his hand and offering up a gleaming smile framed by vibrant green eyes, my knees went gushy and my mind went blank. Should I take this guy seriously? I mean, he was holding a beer in his hands. But it was a light beer, so that's sort of a good thing, right? And the eyes, like beaming lights straight from heaven. Those had to be the real deal.

Like any responsible Christian-camp-recruiting girl, I took his number. I decided to give him a call the next day. Just to see if he remembered talking to me about going to camp—emphasis on *talking to me*. That conversation led to many other late-night conversations and a commitment to recruit some buddies and go to North Carolina to experience the best week of our lives. (As it turns out, it really was the best week of our lives. If for no other reason than because it set a foundation for both the "new guy" and me to really meet Jesus Christ. It was the beginning of a phenomenal relationship. Oh, and for the "new guy" and I as well. More on that later.)

That week, Jesus captured our hearts and allowed us to see that he is relational. He also used this sweet camp experience to bring us together as an official couple. If you ask me, I had scored! I won the boy and grew a little closer to understanding more about everything the Bible has to offer. Our dating life was pretty typical for a normal teenage experience. We went to the movies, rodeos, parties, and school dances. He was my biggest fan, and I was unquestionably his.

I loved decorating his locker before his big football games with good luck signs. He always greeted me in between classes with a quick kiss; he would write me the sweetest love notes telling me how beautiful I was and how much he loved being my boyfriend; he made me feel so special. My walls came down and I fell head over heels in love. Hard. He quickly became my number one priority, which in retrospect, probably was not the best thing. He became someone I couldn't live without; an idol. I am sure a lot of it was about high school romance, but I know that my blind dependence on him was filling the void of love and acceptance from my own home.

His family was an added bonus. His parents were full of life. They were always welcoming and warm. They quickly accepted me as their son's sidekick. They loved unconditionally. There's no question that God brought this boy into my life to show me what unconditional love can look like. It kept me safe from a destructive family dynamic that was unfolding within my own family.

It was my senior year in high school when I decided my feelings for this boy were more than just young love. I had fallen madly in love with him and could not imagine going to a different college and choosing a life that would not have him be a part of it. I think part of my dependence on him and our relationship was that things in my own family were starting to fall apart. My father became unemployed and was out of work for a long time. My brother and sister had gone away to college, so it was just my mom and I to take the brunt of the depression and irritability that began to consume him. My mom had been working as an administrative assistant full time and was doing her best to put her best gloss on our family situation. My dad was intent on maintaining a picture-perfect image. To the outside world, no one knew our financial situation, and my ability to perform in sports and school became a badge for him to wear. With my siblings gone and his eyes on me to be as perfect as possible, I felt so alone.

I guess I cannot blame him for how he loved us. I know it was the only way he knew how. It was how he was raised. What disappoints me is that he couldn't break the cycle of conditional love his parents had used with him. Instead, he continued it with us. As long as I was performing, I was loved. When I was not performing to his standards, there were consequences.

I remember one time I failed to take first place at a track meet. After the meet we drove home in silence. We passed a Church's Chicken, and I asked if we could stop there for dinner. He snapped a vicious retort, "No! If you were skinnier you would have won that race."

Stunned, I sat in the back of his shiny new Chevy Camaro the rest of the ride home with tears streaming down my face. As a young teenager, I took on the self-image that I was fat, insufficient and unworthy. Later, I was nominated to be a part of the Homecoming Court, which was a very big deal at our school. Not having much self-confidence, I was overcome with excitement that my classmates had chosen me to be a part of the homecoming football ceremony. Dressed in a dazzling formal dress, each of the nominated girls were escorted by their dads onto the field to await the announcement for homecoming queen. In that moment, I felt beautiful, accepted, and honored. When one of the other girls was announced as queen, my heart sank. Not because I hadn't won among my friends, but because I knew the shame my father felt. I could feel the tension radiating from him as we slowly stepped off the field, an unsettling experience that only worsened as he gave me the silent treatment for a week following that night. I had failed him. What he did not realize is that the exhausting effort I had put in to being "perfect" at sports, academics and popularity cost me true friendships. I was competitive, shallow, fake, and ruthless. It wasn't because I wanted to be. It was because I did not know how else to gain his favor. I just wanted him to love and accept me for me—but I clearly wasn't enough.

And then it got worse. Still unemployed and depressed, he began to approach me physically in a way that would seem unforgivable to most people. It was a time that made me feel afraid and ashamed. For a number of reasons, I choose not to include the details of this particular time in my life. This is not a story about abuse, it is a store about redemption. For obvious reasons, it had a profound effect on my self-image, my relationships, and my understanding of God. I also think it's important to reach other women out there who may have had similar experiences. I felt shame. I felt alone. I felt despair. But I know now that I was never alone.

That picture-perfect family image had long since evaporated for me and the sadness I felt at watching my father slip into a different identity was heart-breaking. He may not have been perfect in my childhood life, but at least he tried to point our family towards Jesus, if for no other reason than to put on the appearance of doing the right thing in our community. Instead, his heart was consumed by a different idol. He had emotionally and physically damaged me. What's more, he began cheating on my mom. And in one dramatic moment, he decided to turn his back on 28 years of marriage and the family he had built, but could no longer control.

I will never forget the night he left. It was a like great dark cloud had rolled in as a shroud over our house. Looking back there were plenty of signs that our fraud of a family was crumbling. But at that moment, it felt like I was in the fog of a nightmare. The words he spoke were mean, cutting, and heartbreaking. He said he hadn't loved my mom for years. Not since 1980—the year I was born. I asked him if that was when he stopped loving me. He just looked at me with a blank stare and gave no response. His silence was answer enough. When he walked out the threshold of our stained-glass front door, it may as well have shattered when he slammed it behind him. In that moment, the air seemed to suck out of the room. He was gone. He had abandoned all of us.

1. *What were your biggest concerns at this point in your life?*

2. *Who was the most important person you tried to gain approval from and what did you do to gain their approval?*

3. *Did you ever find it possible at this stage in your life that God's plans for you were bigger than your own?*

4. *When did you decide to put your faith and trust and Jesus? Do you remember where you were when the dots connected and you wanted to know him more?*

Chapter 3

Out of the Nest; Adulting?

Outside of my home, I found I was most happy when I was with my boyfriend. He was a year ahead of me in school and when he graduated, he went off to a college in Mississippi. For me, the only logical thing to do was to follow him there once I had graduated. At least if I went to school where he was I knew I could continue pursuing the one relationship that seemed to be working in my favor. He made me feel good. He kept me laughing. He pursued me and always told me how special and beautiful I was to him. I was captivated and at that time in my life, the only thing that seemed to be safe to me was to run at full speed in his direction—and never look back.

Our college experience together was pretty close to picture-perfect. At least, that's how I choose to remember it. We definitely had some highs and lows. We even broke up for about six months to try dating other people. It was more of a challenge to my own misgivings about long-term relationships. After seeing the mid-life crisis my dad had made us live through, I was not sure I could trust men. I came up with this outlandish thought that we needed to try dating someone else to make sure we were really serious about each other. It turned out to be a pretty laughable exercise. Even when we went out with someone else, we instinctively called each other as soon as we would get home from the date and go meet up somewhere to hang out. Obviously, we weren't interested in seeing other people.

It was really at this stage in our relationship that we both realized that the love we had for each other wasn't just an infatuation. It was real. There was a connection between the two of us that could not be broken. Joined at the hip, we spent our weekends attending football games, going to fraternity parties, hanging out with our friends and living the typical college experience. To be honest, we weren't exactly walking with Jesus at this point. He definitely played a role for us, but he wasn't exactly preeminent. I attended a Bible study here or there but still found myself partying on the weekends. We occasionally attended Campus Crusade For Christ events, but never made Jesus a priority.

We spent much more time living the full "college experience" with our fraternities and sororities. I also made a goal to finish college with my boyfriend. It meant I had to really buckle down to gain the hours necessary to graduate a year early. To help pay for my studies, I worked on campus part time. And when I wasn't working or partying, I was in the gym, with what had become a sort of addiction for me: exercise. (Note: I wouldn't exactly say it was a healthy addiction- it helped me pass the time- but it was also my way of holding on to the myth that I had to keep up a good image of myself. Instead of my dad I was trying to perform for, it was my boyfriend.)

I think at this stage in our relationship Jesus knew we would need each other more than we even knew we would. We had a history with each other filled with both fond and difficult memories. We were walking through some pretty deep waters with our families, and we had spent every waking moment together in college, without growing tired of each other. At that time, we traveled back home a lot. My mom was newly single and trying to build a new life. But my boyfriend's mom was also in dire need of support as she was beginning to lose her harsh battle with cancer.

It was in the face of her struggle that we realized we wanted to be married. More than that, we wanted to be married before it was too late for her to be present for the wedding. I still believe God had a way of making the matter urgent for us without sparing the romance of young love. It was not a surprise to me when he proposed, but it was uniquely thrilling and special when it happened. We both felt time pressing us to make a wedding happen, but we relished the excitement of starting a more formal path towards our life together.

I'm going to pause the storyline for a moment to insert a part of this relationship that was crucial to our lives together. His parents. Remember how I said how special they were to me? It's true. They were. But I don't think I ever would have imagined just how important they would have been to me when I was young. I couldn't have seen then just how their unconditional love and acceptance would become a refuge for me. And to this day, I don't know that I ever really let them know just how much they meant to me. I lament that though sometimes because neither of them are here anymore. But God knew what he was giving me when he brought my husband into my life. He not only gave my life partner, he also gave me his siblings and his parents. Parents who would reveal more about the love of Christ to me than a lot of other people in my life, and the funny thing is, they had no idea they were doing it.

When we were dating, both his mother and father always made me feel as if I was one of their own. They were kind, loving and generous. From the very beginning, I was treated as a member of their family. I will forever cherish rib-o-ramas with his dad, bargain shopping with his mom, pork-chop spaghetti dinners, watching movies curled up on their couch, the bear snores we would hear from his dad on the other side of the house when he napped, family trips, and so much more.

But there was a dark side to that as well. Even when both of them faced the diagnoses of terminal diseases, their love still abounded. She would fight ovarian cancer for 11 excruciating years. He was challenged with multiple-sclerosis. For her, cancer was undoubtedly exhausting, but she was always so strong and positive—even when I knew she was in unbearable pain. Looking back, I marvel at how it seemed God had bestowed the fruits of the spirit within her, yet it would still be some time before she had a relationship with him. It's funny how God works within us long before we even realize it. Watching her lose her battle was emotionally and physically draining on us. And yet, through it all, we witnessed grace, joy and miracles as a family. We saw hope in times we didn't think possible. We saw her come to know Jesus as her savior and trust in his provision for her. We saw she and her husband love more deeply through pain and financial strain. It was so hard. But it was also so beautiful.

And then there was her husband, my father-in-law. He was a gentle giant. Sadly, in both spirit and in physical appearance, we watched his body deteriorate with MS. When I first met him, he had such a quick wit and a mischievous nature. But he was kind, and honest, and always wore an infectious smile with radiant blue eyes. I thank the Lord he passed that same smile on to his son; something I treasure to this day. There was only one time I saw him lose his temper. It had something to do with the news of some poor decisions his daughter, the youngest of their three children, had made. He was furious, and I think a little heartbroken. In a rare moment of rage, he took the wine glass in his hand and threw it across the room. I had to duck to the floor to keep it from hitting my head. He didn't mean to throw anything directly at me. His aim was way off (probably because of his MS) and he was just so angry with the choice that his daughter had made that he wanted to throw something. We all stood in shock as the wine in the glass seeped to the floor. Almost immediately he remembered where he was and that his anger was mis-directed. He just chuckled an apology and the matter was over.

I watched him care for his ailing wife while trying his hardest to keep his family together. He never wavered in his love for her or for his family. His later years of life were some of the hardest years for me personally to be around. He had become a dad to me. A dad who accepted me for me.

We were by both of their sides when God called them home. I was 23 when his mom died and 29 when his dad died. One of my greatest gifts was having them both there to give us away at our wedding. To this day I wonder why they both had to suffer through the last parts of their lives. But I do know this, God knew exactly what he was doing, and the reason why they had to become ill and we kids had to witness something so hard to watch at such a young age. From the time of their diagnoses to the moment God called them home I am fully confident in the fact that both of them had fully grasped the grace of Jesus Christ. Losing them made my husband, his brother, and his sister all come to question the bigger picture for their own lives. That picture is still being drawn today, only now it includes Jesus as the as their cornerstone.

Walking alongside your ill or aging parents is not easy. No matter what age or place you are in life. It is just plain hard. But despite this dark cloud, I seemed intent on creating the image of a perfect life. While much of our time was spent caring for his parents, my husband and I feverishly hammered away at making successful careers and starting our own family. I had made a goal for myself to be married, graduated from college, with my first baby be the age of twenty five, and earning six figures before I was thirty. I was well ahead of that game by the time I was 27, and with a second baby and a country-club dream house to add to the tally. From the outside looking in, we had it all. But I will be honest, looking back at that time in my life just exhausts me. The truth is, I felt hollow, empty, alone.

"How?" you may ask. Didn't I have that green-eyed high school sweetheart by my side? My best friend in the whole world? The one I could not live without? Yeah, we were still married. But we were more like two ships passing in the night. Like me, he had also poured himself into a career and he was heroically climbing a gilded ladder. He was enamored with his ever-rising sales commissions and consumed with entertaining clients and traveling the world for fun with friends to hunt, fish, and the like. To be fair, I wasn't giving him much excitement to come home to. I had hammered out my routine to include chasing success at my job just long enough to allow me to hurry home to pour my heart and soul into my babies, whom I had somehow mistaken as the most important idols in my life.

As it turns out, the country club lifestyle we had worked so hard to achieve was the last thing that made me happy. I started to feel resentful. It suffocated me. And instead of directing that toxic feeling towards myself, I directed it towards my husband. He was the one who had left me in this glass castle to maintain and shine—which was no easy task considering I was locked between a schedule of napping children and work deadlines. I began to feel like I had married the wrong man. Even worse, I began to believe it.

I will never forget a visit home to see my mom one weekend. We ran into a family friend whom I had always looked up to. When I told him that it was just me in town for the weekend, he said, "You know your husband is like the Easter Bunny." Not quite grasping his meaning, he continued, "The kind of man that only shows up every once in a while. But even though he's physically there, he's not really there at all." I was stunned by his candor. Sure, it may seem pretty rude to some people. But deep down, I felt a deep pain that informed my soul that this man wasn't being rude, he was being honest. And he could not have been more right. To add to that pain, I realized that if this man, who I seldom ever saw, recognized this reality about us, there were probably many others who did as well. I felt like we were a sham. A lie. It was awful.

I decided right then that something had to change. I realized that I couldn't take the pressure anymore. Propping up an imaginary life of perfection was only following the same path that my father had taken us down years before. I realized that instead of spending my energy being angry at my husband, I could make changes in myself. I chose my career as the first thing to go. My husband wasn't exactly on board. In fact, it took the better part of eighteen months filled with uneasy disagreements before I finally resigned from my job. And even then, it was without his full support. But at that point, I knew it was the right thing to do for us. I was serious about fighting for my family.

Unfortunately, the pressure of being the sole breadwinner in the family made my husband dive even deeper into his job. He worked harder and longer. That meant he was around less and less in my life and the kids'. The storm that was our marriage had escalated to a category four hurricane. He poured himself into work, I poured myself into my kids. I sank deeper into loneliness and self-doubt. And the pain I had felt from my teenage years began to flood my identity. I began searching for answers in all the wrong places.

1. *What good and bad things have you learned about yourself from past relationships?*

2. *Where are you at in your marriage right now? Is there room for growth? Do you have some roadblocks in the way that are holding you back from going deeper with your partner?*

3. *Your family/inlaws- How could you show them you love them even when it may be hard?*

4. *Do you ever wonder what life would be like if you weren't dealt any storms? Imagine how immature your spiritual walk might be if God didn't have you go through things that were difficult.*

Chapter 4

Rain Rain Go Away

It amazes me to see how long a storm can brew in your life without even knowing how bad it really is. My husband and I had on major blinders. Or maybe neither one of us wanted to face the truth. Feeling alienated from him, I began searching for affirmation from an old high school friend who reconnected with me on social media. He never seemed to miss an opportunity to offer me compliments. He repeatedly told me how lucky my husband was to have me. I won't lie, the attention was flattering. So much so that instead of putting a stop to it, I kept coming back for more. It was nice to feel appreciated. Even if it was from the filter of a social media outlet. What started out as seemingly harmless instant messaging turned in to phone calls and conversations that should never have happened. I felt special when talking to this man; like I was beautiful and worthwhile.

And what made me crave his attention was that I didn't have to perform for him like I did for dad, nor did I have to contribute to our financial well-being like I felt I had to do with my husband at the time. I could just be me. While that should have felt like a relief, it also felt horribly wrong. I found myself desiring the affection, but panicking every time I received it. Like a drug, I would tell myself that after this one conversation, I would walk away from it and focus only on my family and my marriage. But somehow, I couldn't do it. The truth is, I was having a full-blown emotional affair with this other man. Even sadder is that I didn't truly feel love for him or anything close to that, but the feelings he gave me were the feelings I felt were void from my marriage.

I began to lie in bed at night wondering how I had could have fallen into this. How could I repeat the same behavior that my dad had done? The behavior that destroyed my family. I could not even swallow the thought that I was doing the one thing to my husband that I swore I would never do after seeing what my dad did to my mom.

Instead of confessing this reality to anyone I buried the secret and pretended everything was just fine. We soon had our 3rd baby and it seemed the Lord began answering some of the prayers I had longed to resolve. Not necessarily in a way that I wanted them answered, but he made it clear he was active in my life. One of my husband's clients at work invited him to a men's Christian retreat. Typically, he would never have entertained an experience like this, but since he stood quite a bit to gain from this client's business relationship, he decided to go. As it turns out, the "big deal" my husband would land as a result of this client's invitation had nothing to do with business at all, but the heart.

That weekend, Jesus came alive in my husband's life. The Holy Spirit revealed a great deal to him that weekend. About his own heart. About his responsibilities as a father and husband. About the fact that I was having an emotional affair. That's right, he said he had a moment of clarity that revealed specific details that led him to know I had sought affection elsewhere. He came home burning to know the truth.

When he came home, I hardly knew how to interpret his transformation. But I did notice something different about the way he looked at me. Just as the Holy Spirit had led him to confront me, he also led me to be ready. Instinctively I found a way to untangle myself from my kids and face him. I was scared. But I felt confident about a reckoning. We were both being guided by something greater than ourselves. We just happened to be there physically.

You know what it's like to watch a big storm brew in the sky? Billowing dark clouds form together. Lightning flashes and thunder cracks and booms. It's a theater that is both frightening and beautiful to encounter. Its luminous light and profound echo seem to be its strongest ingredient. Yet, it's the rain that is the most powerful element. Just before it breaks from the clouds, there's always a stillness. As if God wants everything to be still and silent to prepare for what he wants to reveal. And then, the drops start to trickle down gently. Cold droplets awaken the senses as the storm transitions to a crescendo of torrential rain. Roaring in persistence, its powerful strength is both commanding and cleansing; making new everything it touches. Such is the redemption of Jesus Christ.

That week, the storm of our marriage was cleansed and renewed by his grace. It was one of the hardest and most beautiful weeks of my entire life. It was filled with honesty, sadness, disappointment, listening, compassion, understanding, disgust, and love. As much shame as I had to hide, it felt so good to come clean. I finally had his undivided attention to hear why I was so lonely, lost, and needing his presence in my life. For the first time in our relationship he had ears to hear and eyes to see me in a different light. The scales of judgment to weigh my value and contribution had been removed and he began to see me the way Jesus saw me. I was no longer just his wife and mother of his children. I was a child of God's that had been badly wounded by my earthly father. Those wounds caused me to live out a life I was not proud of pursuing. A life that was seeking others to make me feel loved and validated.

1. *Have you been through a storm and come out on the other side to see God's faithfulness? Or maybe you are going through a storm right now—do you sense his presence?*

2. Can you praise God for the storms you have survived, or are you holding onto bitterness and resentment for the fact that the storm even occurred?

3. Have you experienced the Holy Spirit alive in your life? Can you recognize when he is working?

4. Do you ever doubt God's goodness? I mean, when you are in the midst of the storm it can be easy to doubt, but right now take the time to reflect on seeing where God is/was in the midst of your storm.

Chapter 5

All In

This was a turning point in our marriage and our lives. We sought counsel from our pastor, spent many days at home talking and crying, and finally both started pursuing a life and marriage with Jesus as the center. There was no going back to the mess we had created for ourselves. Our storm had come to a halt. It was like the parable where Jesus silenced a storm with his very own power. He had silenced us. With our emotional walls shaken, and hearts raw, we were listening.

But a heart-felt and repentant apology to my husband was not enough. My heart was compelled to do the same with Jesus. I had felt this shame and disgust weighing me down, but this process remarkably lifted that weight from me. It was unbelievably freeing to surrender; like a great stone had been removed from my chest. What's more, the cleansing of my heart gave me eyes to forgive as well. I forgave those who had hurt me in my past. I forgave my father. I forgave my husband. And I forgave myself.

With a repentant and forgiving heart, my eyes also began to clearly see the trail of lies I had believed about myself for so many years. Those little voices that told me I was fat; I wasn't fast or strong enough; I wasn't smart enough; I wasn't beautiful enough; I wasn't making enough money; I was failing as a mother; I was failing as a wife. They all shouted at me as if I were in a chamber of enemies whose voices would echo in my mind and set my heart racing. Those voices all belonged to one evil spirit: Satan.

All my life I had heard about Satan. I had talked about him in the way you talk about the Boogie Man. I had learned songs about him in Sunday School. Songs like "This Little Light of Mine," where a phrase says, "Don't let Satan blow it out." And "I've Got the Joy, Joy, Joy," where a phrase says, "If the Devil doesn't like it he can sit on a tack." Ouch! Here's the thing. I'm not going to draw up images of some evil spirit out of a horror film. Frankly, I would rather not give him that much attention. But I will say this: Satan is very real. The Bible makes no bones about him. He's mentioned in the first few chapters of Genesis and is referenced 55 times under that name alone thereafter, and he is absolutely the reason our lives on earth are such a mess. If you want to know more, I invite you to read *The Screwtape Letters* by C.S. Lewis for a clear picture of how he best likes to twist our minds and hearts away from Jesus.

Up to that point, I could sum up my life in one, average suburban-girl cliché. The kind of girl that pretended to have life all figured out; too proud to admit any faults or personal failings; too afraid of what others might think of me if they found out what a mess I really was inside. Even worse, I was a "lukewarm Christian," the kind John warns about in **Revelations 3:15–16 when he says, "I know your deeds, that you are neither cold nor hot. I wish you were either one or the other!"**

Do you know how exhausting it is to pretend to be happy? To pretend you are perfect when you know deep down inside you are far from it? I was exactly the sort of fragile soul Satan preys upon. Relatively aware of the grace Jesus had to offer, but too insecure to fully grasp it. Instead I was more amenable to swimming around in my own self-doubt. I began to believe I was not worthy of God's love. (The truth is, I was right about that point of fact, I wasn't worthy. Which is why I needed Jesus. More on that later.) What Satan had me believing was that I had to work to become a child of God, but that I would inevitably fail and never measure up. He had me believing that I was worthless. And I was too weak in my faith to realize that my theology was backwards.

It was at a moment of complete weakness when Jesus came and whispered in my ear. There in my own vulnerability, as my husband and I battled out our own misgivings with each other, I stood at what many might call *rock bottom*. And I had a choice to make: Would I continue to believe the lies, or was I ready to repent, walk away from the sins, and learn to walk in the light that Jesus offers?

It is by God's perfect plan that my husband and I had both come to this stark realization about our lives at the same time. To be honest, I believe it was a gift. In many ways my husband and I were both going through the motions of being adults, but truly we were children. Particularly when you look at it from a spiritual standpoint. We were both moving through our lives with a perspective directed at our own personal gain. Our focus was inward and self-seeking. I say we were children because that's exactly how a child thinks. It is up to a parent to teach them to turn their perspective outward; to not think solely about their self, but to think about others and about what is most important in life. That's what God was doing to us. The truth is, he had desired that of us for our whole life, he just didn't have our attention. Until now. As we rekindled a commitment to our marriage, we also ignited a commitment to Christ; and this time we were supporting each other to keep that mission clear.

1. *What are some areas in your life you give 100%? Parenting, work, marriage, friendships, exercise, health, etc. Where does Christ fit in your daily routine?*

2. *Are any of these areas given more attention than others? In other words, are you out of balance?*

3. *Do you believe that Satan is real, and can you tell when he is attacking you?*

4. *Did you know you can talk to Satan just like you can talk to God? And you have every right to demand that he get out of your life! I shout this to him almost weekly.*

Chapter 6

Relationship Addict

What began to unfold was a dependence on Jesus that I had never really grasped before. I started to take heed in what exactly those words meant. Have you ever stopped to do that? Take a good hard look at what faith is, and what it means to you. I had spent the first part of my life paying lip service to Christianity but not really living a life that reflected a love for Jesus.

II Corinthians 5:17 says "Therefore if anyone is in Christ, the new creature has come: The old has gone, the new is here!"

I had deeply felt the transformation of my heart towards Jesus, but at this very point in my life, it was time that my daily routine began to reflect that. You know that old phrase, "If you're going to talk the talk, you have to walk the walk?" That is exactly what I began doing. I started with simple little changes. It began with the Bible. Instead of simply saying that I believe it was the inspired word of God, but leaving it to collect dust on my bookshelf, I began to open it up. And I began to read it.

I started talking to God like he was right there in the room with me. I began to ask him to reveal himself to me in every part of my life. Even in the deepest, darkest crevices. And bit by bit, I found him.

Jeremiah 29:13 says, "You will seek me and find me when you seek me with all your heart."

I found out that it was true. I felt his presence guide me. I began listening to Christian music while driving in the car. I started working on new friendships that would be positive and fruitful. I relinquished relationships that were toxic and harmful; ones that let my own self-seeking desires flourish. I had to do the steps in order to take away my sinful temptations and stop believing the lies I had allowed to define me.

This process was intentional. Let me repeat that. This was intentional. It took work. Just like any relationship—any *healthy* relationship—I had to invest time and effort into knowing Jesus. (That investment extends to this present day and I pray it will for the rest of my life.) This sort of thing does not happen overnight. This is something I wish someone had told me when I was younger, which is why I want to make it clear to you: Inviting Jesus to be Lord of your life is not a singular event. You don't just say "hallelujah" and expect to be cleansed in eternal perfection like Cinderella by the wave of a wand from her fairy godmother. While it may be nice to experience this sort of fairy tale conversion, it's not exactly how it works. Instead of giving you glass slippers, Jesus hands you a pair of sturdy work boots. And he expects you to get them dirty.

That may sound somehow unappealing. But I promise you, it's invigorating. And it's even addicting. With each new effort I made to follow where he was leading me, I found I craved even more. That's because I was not letting my steps go on a path led by my own shortsighted awareness of life. I was letting go of myself. I was seeing life through His eyes and I began to see really what his most important commandment meant. That commandment is to love. If you read all of the books in the New Testament from John—hint: they all have the word "John" in the title, plus Revelations—you'll find that it's the one word you cannot escape.

John 13:34 "A new commandment I give to you, that you love one another: just as I have loved you, you also are to love one another."

Stop for a moment and read that verse again. See the phrase that says, "As I have loved you?" Think about that for a second. This isn't just a man who walked around earth and said some nice things and gave people hugs and food and went about his merry way. No. This man was fully God. And he left his throne to become one of us. He taught us. He led by example. And then, because he knew that our feeble efforts to follow a bunch of rules would ultimately fail, he decided to do the only thing possible to give us access to his father—God. He died. Here is another one from John:

"For God so loved the world, that he gave his one and only Son, that whoever believes in him shall not perish but have eternal life." John 3:16.

Oh, how that verse gives me chills now that I truly know the depth of what that love means. To Jesus, love meant dying.

Let that soak in.

When he asks us to love one another, as he has loved us, that is a whole lot deeper than … Well, it's pretty deep. It's unfathomably deep. When was the last time you decided to die because you loved someone? It's crazy, right? Guess what? Jesus loves us like crazy. And if he is asking us to love one another like crazy, it means we need to die. We need to die to ourselves; to our passion for self-ambition; to our silly dreams that bring no hope and no real consequence to the world. We need to love without conditions and without strings attached. That's how man does it. That is not how Jesus does it.

Which brings me back to a point about my marriage. To see my husband changed by Jesus and loving me without condition and without strings attached; and to return that love to him—that is a marriage I want to hold on to. But it only works if Jesus is at the center of it.

1. *What are some tangible things you could start doing today to strengthen your relationship with Jesus?*

2. *Are there addictions in your life you need to be freed from?*

3. *Do you really believe and understand how much God loves you, forgives you, and is for you?*

4. *Make a list of the ways you have seen Jesus show you he loves you. Cherish this list and look back at it on your hard days.*

Chapter 7

Surrender Means Freedom

Life with Jesus looks different than a life without him. For one, it is unbelievably freeing. Assuming, of course, you are willing to give up control over your life. I still have my issues. I still sin. All the time. But it is freeing when you can get to a point of giving up full control over all of your situations and allowing the king of kings to take over. But, altogether I know that he works all things for his good, his glory, and his purpose. Relinquishing every aspect of your life over to the God who created everything about you is like throwing a handful of fall leaves from your hands and saying, "Have it all." Saying, "Here is my ugly, my beautiful, and my unmarked territories and I am giving it all to you. Please do what you please and use me for your glory. Take control of my life and show me the way." When you are ready to take this step in your journey you embark on the most beautiful love story imaginable. A love story still written with twists and turns but the villain never wins, the hero always stays the hero and you, my dear, are taken into the story he has always been writing on your life. Are you ready to see this story unfold the way the true author and perfecter of your life intended?

When you are ready for your story to unfold, let Jesus create your heart desires. Let him romance you. Let him desire more of you. Allow the fairy tale story of your own life become a reality. You have probably felt and experienced some of those feelings from everyday relationships, but they come and go, they lose sensation, or they become forgotten. Women want to feel needed. We want to be adored. We live for approval, acceptance, and admiration. That is the way God wired our hearts. Our problem is that we look to fill all of those feelings with earthly people who will fail us at some point in our lives. Because our flesh is weak. All of ours. There is only one perfect person that has ever lived on this earth-Jesus. He is a tenderhearted God who loves us and wants to be in an intimate relationship with us. In **Genesis 2:18, "The Lord God said, "It is not good for the man to be alone. I will make a helper suitable for him."** So God created woman. We are significant in his eyes. We just have to have the understanding that he created us in his image, for his good. Not only did he create us, but he yearns to be in relationship with us. Just like we yearn to be loved by somebody else. **"Now this is eternal life: that they know you, the only true God, and Jesus Christ, whom you have sent." (John 17:3).**

Once I started understanding the depth of Jesus' love for me is when I started to view the Bible as a love story between God and his people. He cares. He has a tender heart and will never give up on loving us. He will pursue us until he calls us home. God longs for us, but he also longs to be loved by us. Culturally we view God as this amazing man who came to save and rescue sinners, but we don't see him as needing anything from us. He wants to be a priority in your life. **Jeremiah 29:13 tell us, "You will seek me and find me when you seek me with all your heart."** The first commandment is to love God. Don't you see, God wants to be wanted? He wants you to put him first in all that you do. Putting your trust and faith in him will drastically change the course of your life. If you are looking to be loved unconditionally, beautifully, intimately and with adventure, then Jesus is the one true God who can fulfill your every desire. **Jeremiah 31:3 "The Lord appeared to us in the past, saying: "I have loved you with an everlasting love; I have drawn you with unfailing kindness."** This is real and this is what true love looks like. Jesus created romance. He created intimacy. He gives us glimpses of his love: everyday-sunsets, the sound of the waves crashing, children laughing, flowers blooming, rivers flowing. He is love. When you make that decision and allow him to be the lover of your soul you will feel whole. You will feel worthy and you will feel adored. You no longer will have to seek others for that approval because you will feel it from your Abba Father.

1. *Are you ready to be more in love with Jesus than with the things of this world?*

2. *What are some of the things of this world that are holding you back from giving your entire life over to Jesus? Remember you can't have one foot in and one foot out in order to grow.*

3. *Do you understand following him comes with a price? What might you lose to gain more of him?*

4. *Can you live with those things you might lose knowing you have gained an eternal relationship with Jesus?*

Chapter 8

Change Is Good

For my husband and I, our story had a new beginning. Jesus had restored our marriage and refocused our mission together. My focus had to become solely on pursuing a life with Jesus. I discovered the verse in **Matthew 16:25** where Jesus says that**, "For whoever wants to save their life will lose it, but whoever loses their life for me will find it."** It was no longer me that would be in control of every choice and situation. I was freely giving it to my Eternal Father who I now looked up to and wanted him to be the author and perfecter of my life.

I noticed a transformation in my husband as well. Instead of watching mindless television before bed, he began reading his Bible. Instead of spending evenings entertaining brokers and hanging out with his friends, he stayed home with his family. He shared his struggles with me in determining which relationships he needed to remove himself from that were not honoring to God. He also insisted we make church a priority. God was molding him and our entire family just like I had always dreamed of. The model my father had given me was a fraud, but God knew that I needed a man that actively pursued Jesus and lived a life that mirrored the heart of Christ.

Conversations changed between the two of us. Suddenly, we had ears to hear one another, to dig deeper into what was in each other's hearts and minds. We would confess to each other our daily struggles. And we began to pray for one another. He also began praying out loud with our children. We went from wanting to be known to wanting to know Jesus. We stopped caring about being in the right crowd or accumulating things and focused more on serving others. We hated how so much of that life we were chasing had still left us feeling empty. We openly talked about keeping each other accountable to keep from falling back into that self-centered lifestyle. And we were quick to notice when Satan was lurking and made sure to put on our full armor of God and not let Satan win.

We also found that our parenting became different. Instead of making sure we were invited to all the right birthday parties, or had the best toys, we just decided to hunker down as a family unit, building up our family relationships. Of course, we still remained social, but we became more deliberate about the relationships we fostered. We actively pursued others that we knew were also pursuing a life with Jesus. We needed positive Christian influences around us to help guide us, encourage us, and pray for us. We made intentional time to invest in each of the kids separately by creating date nights with them. This time has allowed us one on one time to make memories together and build confidence in our love for them. Our hope was that it would teach them a thing or two about what dating should look like as they got older.

I also began journaling for my children. Each child was given their own journal and I began writing to them during the day when they were away at school. As part of their bed time routine they would write me back. It has been one of the sweetest ways for me to personally connect with them on a deeper level. So much has been revealed to me through their writing and in return I have been able to write Biblical truth and encouragement to them that they can read now and look back at later.

Bottom line, we stopped trying to shape a "cookie cutter" image of how our culture expected our lives to be. Instead, we were pointing our goals towards Jesus. I am not sure if our marriage would have been saved if only one of us was committed to walk this journey with Jesus. It is truly by the grace of God that he wove our hearts for him together as one. I have learned that marriage is sacred and one of the greatest gifts God has given us. Loving your spouse is not the end goal. It is the byproduct of a growing relationship with Jesus Christ. Fixing our eyes on him mends your heart, your mind, and your relationships. That simple pivot to give it to Jesus is the best marriage therapy you can get. For marriages that are crumbling apart, a counselor is always helpful, but you have to seek the "Wonderful Counselor," as Isaiah 9:6 describes him, as your first priority. I also learned from Ruth Graham Bell that "A happy marriage is the union of two good forgivers." Both my husband and I were willing to forgive our wrong doings and work at making things right again.

1. *List some practical examples of how you could spend more quality time with your husband and your children.*

2. *How do you think your kids will respond if they see you making more effort to really know them?*

3. *Are you willing to make changes with your family life in order to grow closer together?*

4. *Are you and your spouse on the same page about making positive changes that will help everyone in your family grow closer to the Lord and closer as a family?*

Chapter 9

God's Not Finished

Growing up I had a sign in my bathroom that said, "Please be patient God isn't finished with me yet." I never understood how true that was until I started to see real transformation happening in my own life. Even though I recognized my heart change was happening and it was obvious I was walking with the Holy Spirit, I still doubted my ability to be used by God to help others. By surrendering our marriage, we began to see Jesus move in our hearts. I began to see a new illustration of how Jesus brings us into his presence. It materialized as the image of adoption. Ever since the fall of man in the Garden of Eden (Genesis 3), humans have been separated from God. We have walked this earth either trying to follow him or fleeing from him. But despite our sin and fallibility, he still seeks our hearts; he still longs for us to be with him. And it's not like we are these shiny new babies wrapped in a blanket and left on the door step by the stork.

By the time many of us truly accept Christ into our lives, we are pretty ugly, beaten and even hard to love.

But the idea of adoption is the true story of the Gospel. Adoption often involves a price; a tradeoff of something to take one being and make him your own. When God sent his son, he sent him to die, not so that he might be a martyr, but as ransom for our iniquity. As the price to pay for us to become his family. The great adoption is about our salvation.

Having experienced this redemption in our lives, my husband and I began to feel a call to look at adoption within our own family. It was not a light decision. We were already a family of five, the youngest of which was only 2 years old. But the impact of the grace that had been given to us began to weigh heavy on our hearts. We researched the possibility, prayed heavily over it, and sought counsel from friends and family. In the end, we didn't feel we were equipped to do all that was involved in the foster family process. At the same time, we agreed to keep an open mind to the prospect if God gave us a clear direction. We committed to be obedient to his calling.

Well guess what, he gave us a clear direction.

As my husband quietly listened to his coworker share the whole story, he prayed with her and told her we had just been through a foster training and could help answer questions or even help if she ever needed it. Three weeks after their conversation his co-worker called us back the night of my 33rd birthday. We both knew she wasn't calling about work. We sat on the back porch sipping a glass of wine and listened to her tell us the latest mishaps with the baby and baby-mommy and daddy. And then … this grandma of the baby asked us if we would consider taking care of this precious baby while the parents went and got help. There was never much discussion after that night. My husband and I just looked at each other with tears in our eyes as we both agreed that helping this family was the right thing to do. We could not even believe that God chose us to be a part of her story and were even more astounded at the fact that he thought we were capable of doing something for the kingdom. We were asked to fill in the gap for a precious baby girl that desperately needed a forever family. A family that would fight for her, raise her, love her, and point her to knowing all about him.

This was a clear communication from God that when you ask him to move in your life, he moves fast! And a great understanding for me to fully grasp how we hear from the Lord. It wasn't through an audible voice or even a dream. It was through other people and circumstances. God is so intentional. If only we be still and alert to seeing him work. We knew that this would be a big test of our faith. We prayed about this precious little baby. Should we walk in obedience and trust his plan for our family and this baby? Or would we allow fear to creep in and paralyze us from experiencing his goodness and his constant pursuit on each of our lives in the process? We talked it over with our other kids. We sought prayers from friends and family. But truly, from the first moment we heard about her, we knew the only answer was to bring her home to us.

Literally three days after we said yes, a four-week-old baby girl was delivered to our home. In those three days before we met her, we busily readied our family, our home, and our hearts. I witnessed community come together the way I read about in the Bible. Friends, family, and neighbors heard we were getting a baby and within hours I had a crib, car seat, baby clothes, diapers, mattresses for my other girls, and anything else this baby could possibly need. I witnessed what it meant to be the hands and feet of Jesus when I saw my community come around our family to support and welcome this sweet little girl.

Over the first days and weeks we fell in love with her. And through intentional prayer for her parents' healing we even began to fall in love with her parents. We didn't judge them for their wrong choices or get angry for not fighting to keep their baby. I remember struggling with the fact that I was so grateful to help save this baby but worried about who could save these young parents. They desperately needed guidance, unconditional love, and a lot of healing. We visited the father in prison. Our children learned what a pen pal was and loved receiving letters from the biological father. We would write him back sending encouragement and scriptures. I mean we are talking serious conversations with our young kids about how to accept others who are different from us, and how to pray for those who are hurting the ones we love. So many hard yet deep and powerful life lessons we were able to bring our children alongside us with on this journey. We did the same for the mother as well, praying that Jesus might stir in her heart and that someone would come into her life to help her. I loved for this baby to be saved, and I also longed for the biological parents to be rescued by our ultimate healer.

That was not an easy year. And I am not just talking about rejoining the world of changing diapers and mid-night feedings. It was an emotional roller coaster as well. We were technically fostering this child. We very quickly realized that adopting her was our end goal. But the tumultuous process of court dates introduced anxiety that I had never experienced before. During this time, the father had signed away his rights to her, but the mother had not. She was required to appear before a judge and clear a drug screen multiple times throughout a twelve-month cycle.

This baby had woven herself into the fabric of our family, and we loved her dearly, yet with each new court date I had to prepare my heart that she could be taken away from me. Most of those dates came and went with relief each time the mother failed to appear. But at one point, she did appear. And she did say she still wanted to try to keep her. I will never forget the fear that overwhelmed my body. Would God really do this to me? Would he really ask me to love and nurture a baby and bring my other kids into the mess of a story just to take her away from us after a year? All I could think about was the complete devastation and sadness it would bring to all of us. It was at this moment that God spoke to me very clearly one early morning through my prayer time. He told me that all children are his children. He asked me to be the mom to each of them and to fully trust his plan in each of their lives that he has already mapped out for them.

I was not supposed to save this baby. That was not my job. That was God's job. I just needed to be obedient and ready for whatever he threw my way. I still think relinquishing complete control over to someone else (in this case I chose God to be that someone else) is somewhat scary and freeing all at the same time. And isn't it a profound illustration of how God asks us to trust him completely? So often, we hold on so tightly to the things we want, hoping to manage and control things. Yet, God has a funny way of showing us exactly who the author is writing this story—of course, at the time, I definitely didn't find it funny.

My faith felt challenged. We had obeyed God's calling to open our home, yet we were living on a virtual yo-yo of instability, not knowing if she would one day be ours permanently.

Isn't that a profound illustration? How we can be driving to want to love and care for something so much, yet not be sure that we will actually get to? Isn't that how God pursues us? Fortunately, God has the benefit of omniscience, meaning he ultimately knows if our hearts will choose him, but it doesn't make the heartache any less great for him.

It was during this year that God started to reveal to me how much I desperately needed him; every hour of every day. Not just in the mornings and evenings and on Sundays. I was calling on him almost hourly in complete fear, lack of control, and utter amazement at each new detail that would unfold. And you know what? Jesus met me every single time

I called upon his name. He calmed my nerves; reassured me we were doing the right thing; showed me the baby was where she needed to be; and gave me signs of his presence.

I knew God had this baby girl's life in the palm of his hands. He taught me that she was his, and I was just chosen to be a part of her story he had already woven together. It became very clear to me at this stage in my walk with the Lord that as long as I was going to allow him to be the author of my life, he was going to continue to write a beautiful love story that I would get to share with those that wanted to hear.

Hebrews 12:2 tells us, "fixing our eyes on Jesus, the pioneer and perfecter of faith. For the joy set before him he endured the cross, scorning its shame, and sat down at the right hand of the throne of God."

Jesus guides our faith, presides over it, and cares for it all the days of our lives.

1. *What experiences in your life can you look back at where it was obvious God was involved in every single detail?*

2. *Did those experiences force you to need Jesus more?*

3. *Can you grasp the magnitude of his sovereignty in your life and allow him to take the lead in the driver's seat?*

4. *Are there areas in your life that you know you need to let go of so that God can move? What is holding you back from giving those over to the best storyteller there is?*

Chapter 10

Dear Bio Mom

Dear Bio Mom,

I cannot believe five years ago this week was the day your daughter became my daughter, too. Never in a million years did I think adoption was even in my path, but I am so thankful God opened my eyes to caring for orphans. It wasn't until I realized that I too was an orphan and Jesus Christ came to rescue me that I wanted to rescue someone else. Something in my heart changed forever when I understood that my eternal Father came to save and love me unconditionally. I no longer saw myself as this shameful and abandoned girl who could never walk with her head held high. I finally felt unconditional love from someone who would never turn their back on me. It allowed me to open my heart to the idea of showing one of his own children that same kind of agape love.

There are so many things I want you to know about your daughter. She exudes joy. Pure and undefinable joy. She is smart and loves learning. She gets so excited when she learns something new and wishes school was every day of the week. She is social and fun to be around. She prefers when lots of children are around to play with over a quiet home with just me. She attracts people around her because she is so stinkin' cute. Her big brown eyes and contagious smile light up any room that she walks into. She has a quick temper that comes out occasionally, but I can't help but laugh because she looks and acts like a lion on the prowl. It's actually kind of cute. She loves singing songs and is obsessed with anything Frozen. Elsa is her favorite princess and she has even tried to convince some of her playground teachers or people we meet that her name is Elsa. And if I don't pretend to be Anna and play back with her that lion prowl goes into full attack. She loves egg tacos, avocados, bananas with peanut butter, and Hershey's kisses. If I can't find where she is, the first place I look is the driveway because she is probably out riding her bike while wearing her ladybug princess dress. She wears that thing every single day. She also loves reading books before bed and has just started demanding a hug and a kiss before she falls asleep. I am sure her reasoning is to stall before bed, but I like to think maybe she just loves to come and give me hugs and kisses. She is a literal thinker. Often times when I try to explain that Jesus is always with her she looks around the room and shouts back at me that she can't see him anywhere. I know one day she will understand. How could she not? I mean Jesus has written such an amazing story on her heart.

This girl is a true gift and a tough one to reason with, but my goodness, every day that she tests my buttons all I keep thinking about is the sacrifice that Jesus did for me up on that cross. Then I think about the sacrifice you did when you signed your rights away to me five years ago. Then I remind myself that I can handle the sacrifice I chose. She is worth it. Sometimes I wonder if you even know about the sacrifice that Jesus did up on that cross. It was for you, too. I wonder if you believe that you are worth it. Periodically, I find myself searching the internet and Facebook to see if I can find any update on your whereabouts. I pray for you and wonder how you are. I will never forget how much my heart broke as I sat across the table from you when our daughter was eleven months old. My flesh wanted to be so mad at you for the poor choices you were making, but my soul wanted to swoop you up into my arms and take you home to rescue you, too. I would lay in bed at night wondering who and how I could find someone that could take you in and care for you, too. Someone to show you what unconditional love looked like. I knew your story. I knew how badly your daughter needed to be rescued, but I also knew that you needed the same thing. The generational sin that you were enslaved to was too thick for you to even know how to break the cycle. Oh, how that broke my heart and still breaks my heart today.

It was five years ago that I got the honor of becoming a mom again to a darling four-month-old baby girl. Five years ago that changed the course of how I choose to live my life. Five years ago that allowed me to meet Jesus in a new and deeper way than I ever imagined was possible. Five years ago that my family was now considered a large family. Five years ago that I would experience what sacrificial love really looks like. Five years ago that God gave me eyes to see brokenness in someone besides myself. Sympathy instead of judgment. Love instead of hate. Pain instead of pride. I pray you are out there somewhere making something of the life you have been given. I pray you come to know Christ and experience joy and peace for the first time in your life. I pray that you know how loved you are by a forgiving Father who wants you to fall into his arms and never look back. I pray this for you and I pray it daily over our daughter. The daughter that you brought into this world and the one I get the privilege to raise. I promise to do my best to give her everything she needs both emotionally and physically. I promise to always tell her who you are and how much you loved her. And I promise to always have a listening ear or a welcoming heart if you ever want to reach out to meet her again. Oh, how I dream about sharing Jesus with you one day. Thank you for caring so much about her that you entrusted me with her. Thank you for choosing life.

Love,

Your daughter's other mother

Chapter 11

Mom Guilt

Parenting four children of all different ages and personalities is quite a task. I am not quite sure how I manage to keep up with their schedules, homework load, meals, playdates and activities. I often wonder if I am meeting all of their emotional needs; and I often worry whether or not I am failing them big time. The role of a mom is both daunting and fulfilling. Every day I experience highs and lows. Every day I question my job. But every day Jesus reminds me that he has me right where he wants me.

It should be no surprise to the people who know me that I definitely fall in the category of having a "type A" personality. I like to get things done. I am organized, driven, focused, involved, social, and persistent. I have spent years trying to convince myself that being a stay-at-home mom is what is best for my family. Yet, I still struggle with it. I know that being a mom is the most important job the Lord will ever bless me with. But sometimes I feel that I could be doing so much more. In my head, I realize there is no such thing as "just being a mom." It is perhaps the most important job anyone can be gifted with. I get that. But I struggle with whether or not it's enough. We live in a culture where women live under a great deal of pressure to be educated, be married, be a mother, and have a great career. It's the American Dream, right? I have to admit this is one issue in my life that I have waves and flows of being at peace with staying home and not being at peace for staying home. I often wonder if maybe the lack of peace is because God is slowly stirring my heart for something more. Or maybe I am just not content. Each day my feelings on this particular issue wavers but one thing remains the same. The ultimate truth that God loves me. He is for me, and he will bring me new ideas or new opportunities when the time is right.

During this daily dependence I have chosen in Christ, I know he has me right were he wants me and that his plan for me is sufficient. Yet I still struggle with this thing called mom guilt. Whether I stay home or work, I feel guilty. Whether I make money or spend money, I feel guilty. Whether I leave my kids with a sitter or go on a date night, I feel guilty. Whether I leave my kids with a sitter or go on a date night I feel guilty. My heart is pulled in so many different directions. And I know how badly I need to invest in other things besides my kids. Like my marriage. It needs to be at the top of that list. What I have discovered is that it really does not even matter what I decide to do that day. I will either be overwhelmed in guilt or overwhelmed in peace that I am following God's lead and that I am trusting where he takes me. I wish I could tell you that I always trust and I never feel guilty but that is just a big fat lie. The struggle is real. Almost daily. Mom guilt is real.

But there is nothing about that struggle that shows a dependence on God. What it reveals is that I still manage to let Satan's lies seep into my brain. The truth is, when I take a deep look at my life now and reflect on what my job description consists of, I realize I am running a company; a household of a large family, with busy schedules for four children. And I have the opportunity to influence my kids in the best way that I can. This profound way of looking at my life has also shown me that my occupation is my mission field and my purpose is to be like Jesus.

If I have the right outlook on my role at home, I can treat it just like I would any other thriving career. I can give 100%. I can manage my life and my children's lives with the help of the best boss I could ever imagine—Jesus. He can give me direction and lead the path. I just have to obey and follow him daily. My role as mom allows me to enter the mission field every morning when I wake up. How will I portray who Jesus is to my children? How will I serve my husband well? How will I accomplish all the tasks in the day with a servant heart?

The reward may not come in the currency of a big hefty pay check, but it pays hefty dividends every time I hear the words "thank you," or "yes, sir/ma'am," or when I see them look an adult in the eye, or show respect towards others. I recognize them gaining self confidence in who God made them to be.

Romans 12:2 tells us, "Do not conform to the pattern of this world, but be transformed by the renewing of your mind. Then you will be able to test and approve what God's will is–his good, pleasing and perfect will."

Whether you work full time, part-time or stay home with your kids, we are all moms. And we all have a job at home that is the most important job we will ever have in our career path. Look at where God has you and remember that your job is your mission field. Wherever you are throughout the day, whether it is in meetings, in front of a computer, building blocks on the floor with your toddler, or at school serving and volunteering, remember that your purpose is to be like Jesus in all that you do.

1. *Do you struggle with guilt because you work? How does it affect your job tasks and attitude at work?*

2. *Do you struggle with guilt because you decided to be a stay at home mom? How does this affect how you live at home and how you treat your children or your spouse?*

3. *What other areas of mom guilt do you experience? (ex: when I go on a date I feel guilty hiring a babysitter-time away from them and money spent when I didn't work to earn any of the money)*

4. *How can you eliminate feeling guilty for living the life God has given you? Remember he has you here for a reason!*

Chapter 12

Parenting Is Just Plain Hard

So let me just be really honest. Parenting a toddler for the 4th time is harder than it ever was before. I have never been a huge fan of the childhood stage of about twenty months to four years old. Sure, I love seeing their personalities come out and watching them discover the world with such naive lenses. I love their laughter, their need for hugs, and their excitement over the little things. It is a sweet time and I try my hardest to soak it all in. And believe me I know—they grow up so fast. But at this particular stage where reason bears no weight, whining is at an all-time high, and having a complete adult conversation at one time is pretty much impossible. And let's not forget the harrowing task of potty training. My least favorite stage of parenting. Oh, and don't forget that toddlers require naps; which slows your busy mom schedule down.

Having a toddler with three older kids—all with myriad activities and school commitments—means a regular routine is hard to pin down. Instead, we divide and conquer and do the best we can; which sadly means our family is rarely together as a whole.

I want to be clear that despite the general exhaustion of managing a chaotic family life, I have never once regretted bringing our fourth child into our home. In fact, it's quite the opposite. Every day I see how much she has blessed our lives, our family, and our faith. And bit by bit, God has revealed to me why he gave her to me when he did. He knew she was just what I needed in order to grow with him. Having her has forced me to be still, be quiet, and to grow to a deeper relationship with Jesus. I have had to say "no" to a lot of doing for others and I have learned to say "yes" to being home even though that was not what I thought I would be doing at this stage in my life with my other children. For this gift, I am eternally grateful.

Parenting is hard, and it is exhausting. And I know I am not alone. Whether you are a stay at home mom, or a mom juggling a full-time job with a family, or a single mom working two jobs, just know that you are not alone. Parenting is just plain hard. Especially for those of us that are really trying to have some skin in the game and try to raise our kids up in the way they should go. And there is nothing more revealing about your true self than having kids run you ragged to start scratching away that shiny veneer you've had lacquered on your life when you thought you and everything else was just perfect.

I share this with you because it is honest. More importantly, I share it with you because this is where Jesus meets you. At our lowest moments of self-pity and frustration, it is our own hearts that are whining and complaining and begging for an escape, and that is when Jesus rolls us his sleeves, gets right down on the floor with our worn out bodies, props up our weary faces and says, "I love you."

Yet again, this season of parenting is a clear illustration of God's role in our lives as our Father. Plenty of times we have whined, complained, fought, and even thrown all-out tantrums about the circumstances in our lives. But his love never waivers. For all the times he should have thrown up his hands and sought an escape from our childish ways, he always remains constant.

I Corinthians 13:4–8 "Love is patient, love is kind. It does not envy, it does not boast, it is not proud. It does not dishonor others, it is not self seeking, it is not easily angered, it keeps no record of wrongs. Love does not delight in evil but rejoices with the truth. It always protects, always trusts, always hopes, always perseveres. Love never fails. But where there are prophecies, they will cease; where there are tongues, they will be stilled; where there is knowledge, it will pass away."

Remember that, the next time you invite yourself to your own pity party—I often do. His love never fails. What a good Father, he is.

1. *Are you doing your job that you have been given to the best of your ability for the glory of the Lord?*

2. *Have you examined where you are at in your life and come to grips that God has you where you need to be? Or are you sensing he may be urging you to make a change?*

3. *What mom guilt do you struggle with most?*

4. *Are there ways to help eliminate the mom guilt so that you can be more in the moment and not overcome with guilt?*

Chapter 13

#StillBeingTested

Walking out a Christian life still has its challenges. Just because I am all in with Jesus doesn't mean life is easy. Here are just some of my daily struggles I still battle yet at least I know now that God is on my team. Just trying to keep it real and help you understand that choosing a life with Jesus doesn't solve all of your worldly problems. It simply helps you put your problems into a deeper perspective and learn to laugh at things a little bit more. God is still testing me and I am up for whatever he may throw my way.

Sometimes I pretend to be asleep at night so that I don't have to do bedtime routine every single night #WHENWILLTHEYPUTTHEMSELVESTOBED

There are days when I just need a break from my toddler so I take her to the kids club to play with her friends and then just sit in my car alone for an hour #MUCHNEEDEDBREAK

I told my daughter that I had a terrible and contagious rash just so I could take a bath alone for once #NEVERDOANYTHINGALONE

I poured a bottle of cold water on my daughter's head to get her to stop crying, and I didn't feel bad about it at all. I laughed harder than I've laughed in a long time #BADMOMPROBLEMS

I have started eating a bowl of cereal in private around 4:00 in the afternoon because it's likely the meal I prepare for dinner will be eaten by my kids with nothing left for me #BIGFAMILYPROBLEMS

I always eat the last brownie and blame it on their dad #BEMADATDAD

It brings me unspeakable joy when I get to embarrass my son at school #HEWILLLAUGHLATER

I've started telling my daughter my neck is broken so that I don't have to hold her everywhere we go. Sometimes she feels sorry for me #LITTLEWHITELIES

I am a firm believer that year-round school would make me a better mom #SIGNMYPETITION

I have offered some pretty unrealistic bribes in order to get my toddler to poop in the potty and I still don't know how I am going to make any of them happen when she finally succeeds #RIDEAPURPLEHORSE

I keep thinking maybe I should let go of all of the control and let the kids eat whatever they want and do whatever they want for a whole 24 hours but the aftermath of that idea scares me too much #LETITGO

I love being a mom and wouldn't want to be doing anything else but I also daydream my next big business ideas all the time still hoping one day my big ideas will come to fruition #DAYDREAMER

9 times out of 10 I call my kid by the wrong name #TOOMANYKIDS

I often look to a stranger during my kid's tantrums and tell them to get their kid under control #MYKIDWOULDNEVERDOTHAT

After catching my daughter lying one too many times, I punished her by making he wear her brother's clothes to school #SCARREDFORLIFE

My youngest child packs her own lunch for preschool and I'm quite certain it includes 2 bags of Cheetos and chocolate chips #ORGANICFORFIRSTBORNSONLY

I sometimes have to google answers to my elementary age kids' homework: Does this count as being resourceful or stupid? #MOMSMARTS

I skip over paragraphs at a time when reading a bed time story to my young ones: At least I am still spending time and reading with them. #IJUSTWANTTOGOTOBED

I spy on my daughter when she has friends over. #YOUKNOWYOUDOTOO

I finely chop vegetables to sneak them into many meals. #JUSTTRYINGTOHELP

I have convinced my children that trampoline parks are dangerous and someone gets hurt every single day there so it isn't a place we can go. #FEAROFINJURIES

I spoiled Christmas and told my 2 older kids that Santa wasn't real and their reaction to the news brought me much laughter. #SANTAISFAKE

I have stashed my kids' birthday money away that was given to them and later pulled it out for us to eat or grab a snack after school. #SHARETHEWEALTH

When my kids get too many presents for their birthday or Christmas from extended family I quickly and quietly hide the presents in my attic and pull them out the next year #REGIFTER

I am not ashamed to buy used toys from the garage sale site to give as Christmas presents #CHEAP

When my kids were little and couldn't read a clock, I used to rush them through the bed time routine and tell them it was almost midnight to get them in bed as quickly as possible so that I could have some peace and quiet in the house: Little did they know it wasn't anywhere close to midnight. More like 8:30-9:00. #INEEDMYBEAUTYSLEEP

Sweet and hard working mommas: I know I am not the only one who has similar stories. Don't feel bad about it. Never doubt your role as a momma. Do what you have to do and be the best momma you can be to your little ones. Remember most of all that why we do what we do is because we love our children and that is what matters. God is on your side and with him your outcome is sure to be a winning team!

Psalm 127:3 "Children are a heritage from the Lord, offspring a reward from him."

Chapter 14

Faith Journey

I often wonder what it will take for God to capture the heart of each of my kids. I pray daily that they will one day own their own faith and taste just how sweet he is. I even ask God to break them down while they are still living under my roof so that we can help guide them to the truth of who God says they are. I know they are going to be faced with a lot of temptations, pressures, and expectations. The reality is that they cannot live under this bubble of our safe home for as long as they live. At some point they are going to have to learn to stand on their own two feet and own their own faith. The thought of that frightens me. It is a daunting task to think of how important of a role model and truth speaker I am as their mother. Will they believe all the scriptures I point them to? Will they hold on to the stories in the Bible that I try to make relevant in their lives today? Will they start a relationship with Jesus without me reminding them to pray, go to church, or do their Bible study? When will something in them click so that they are all in for Jesus just like I am? I want this so so badly for each of my kids. And the truth is, it is not up to me to make this happen. It isn't on my agenda nor is it my full responsibility. God is bigger than me and I know he has each of my kids in the palm of his hands. Their story is his story and I just pray that I can be a seed planter that helps point them in the right direction to truly know him.

This past week we had the opportunity to welcome home an orphan from Ethiopia. We have prayed for this particular boy and his family for six years. The day had finally come that they would get to bring him to their own home and back to our community. We were so excited to see God's faithfulness in the entire process. The night that they were to be arriving home by plane my kids begged to go to the airport with their friends to celebrate this little boy's arrival. Honestly, I was not in the mood to go. The traffic would be bad, my husband was leaving town, and I still knew I had the nightly duties of homework, bath, and dinner. I mustered up some energy and a change of heart because I wanted to support our friends and, oh my word, I am so glad that I did! God showed up in a huge way! In a way I didn't see coming.

As the family came down the escalator with their new son in tow we all cheered and cried as we celebrated them all being home as a family. It was beautiful. Community came together and you could just tell how many faithful prayer warriors were a part of this little boy's journey to get to his forever family. As everyone gathered around to hug and welcome them home, my twelve-year-old son (who is almost as big as me) was literally weeping the biggest crocodile tears I have ever seen him cry in my entire life. Uncontrollable crying as he stood close to me and just watched this celebration take place. At one point I asked him if he was okay because he seriously couldn't stop crying, and he just smiled really big and gave me a thumbs up. The crying continued as we snapped pictures with everyone. I even had a few other mothers ask me if he was okay or if he wasn't feeling well. I was actually a little embarrassed for him as I watched him struggle to keep his emotions under control. It wasn't until we left the scene to walk back to our car that he started to get himself together again. The car ride home was chatty in the back with my three girls but my son remained silent. I decided to take them to dinner since it would be too late to cook. We sat down to eat and my son finally decided to talk. The first thing he said was, "That was the happiest moment of my life." A little taken back (because let's face it … I am his mom and I can think of a million other times he's been really happy). I asked him why that moment was so happy and he said, "Mom, can't you see? We just welcomed home this little boy. He's been adopted into a forever family." My response, "Yes, babe you are right. And what you just witnessed is a tangible picture I believe the Lord gave you tonight for two reasons. It was a small glimpse into the reality of how much Christ and all of his believers celebrate when you chose a life with him. See son, you too, are adopted. And your Heavenly Father rejoices the moment you decide you want to be a part of his forever family. Not only that son, but remember the picture of welcoming home you saw tonight. Don't forget it either.

Because the moment you take your last breath and enter into the gates of Heaven, just imagine all of the angels gathered around Jesus to welcome you home forever."

This was one moment I believe that will be life changing for my son. The tangible picture God gave him will stay with him forever. See, I realize that living out our faith allows our kids to grab hold of what we believe in. And in doing so we get to take a ride alongside them as they live out their own faith journey. A journey that I pray will draw them closer to Christ and deeper in love with what really matters.

Ephesians 1:5 "He predestined us for adoption to sonship through Jesus Christ, in accordance with his pleasure and will."

1. *What are some ways you can start living out your faith today?*

2. *Living out your faith for your kids is the best way for them to want the same thing in their life. Remember the best way to disciple them is caught not taught. Write down things you can do to help connect the dots for your children to grasp how deeply loved they are by their maker.*

3. *What bible verse can become your family verse? One that you all learn and decide to make your mission, your heart's desire. Write it on the tablet of your heart and live by it DAILY.*

4. *Are there opportunities you and your family could be missing out on being involved in that could eternally impact the view your kids have about Jesus?*

Chapter 15

My Father

"I learned that who doesn't look for you, doesn't miss you and who doesn't miss you doesn't care for you ... that destiny determines who enters your life but you decide who stays ... that the truth hurts only once and a lie every time you remember it. There are three things in life that I leave and never return: words, time and opportunities ... Therefore, value whoever values you and don't treat as a priority whoever treats you as an option." (picture quote)

Well, this quote hit me like a ton of bricks. I have been wrestling for the last twenty years of my life about how, when, and if I should be trying harder to restore a relationship with my estranged dad. I can't believe twenty years have passed and I have only seen him a handful of times at a funeral and twice because we actually tried.

My parents divorced when I was eighteen. I never saw it coming. Everything that transpired over the course of the divorce was so hurtful, so hard, and so raw. I am finding it still hurts today. I have totally forgiven my dad for the ways he left our family. I have forgiven him for the hurt he caused my mom, my brother, my sister, and me. I have grown from the pain he put me through, and I have learned what an unhealthy relationship can look like. But something I still struggle with today is whether or not I should be trying harder and doing more to have him back in my life.

Now that today is here, I struggle with questions like: Should I work at having a relationship with my dad? Why do I have to be the one to initiate the process? When he calls me why does it feel so awkward? Is twenty years too long to try and repair a relationship? What do I talk to him about? Do I let him know who my kids are? How can I trust him? He is the adult in this relationship, so why is he not making an effort? Why did he give up on me? Will I regret not knowing him as I grow older? Why do I put the guilt and shame all on me for things that happened between us? What do I do when my kids ask to know him?

I love my dad. I love him dearly. I had a wonderful childhood with fabulous memories. I am thankful for the family I grew up in. But the reality of what happened to me during my teenage years and the abandonment I have always felt since he walked out on my family still makes me feel empty sometimes.

I wavered between sharing my heart and being honest with him or burying it under the rug and moving on. I mean,

I think I have dealt with the situation on my own. I am positive I no longer live with bitterness or anger. I know I am living in a freedom that only God can give. But is this all that God has for me? Or does more freedom await? Does this one giant turn of events on my life really need to be addressed in order for me to go deeper with my eternal Father?

As I contemplated what to do, my body tensed up, and I felt the Spirit nudging me to go deeper. Don't hold back. Don't live with regrets of not getting things off your chest. But, I hate confrontation. Who wants to relive their past when their past wasn't something worth wanting to remember anyhow? I had to remember that the only one worthy of condemning us is the only one who chose to forgive us. But when the Holy Spirit nudges us to confront someone who has messed up, we should do so with honesty, compassion, and humility. Our main motive behind confronting them should be to bring restoration. **Matthew 18:15 "If your brother or sister sins, go and point out their fault, just between the two of you. If they listen to you, you have won them over."**

I finally mustered up the nerve to confront my earthly dad. I knew I could not keep holding in the hurt any longer. I felt like I owed it to him to understand why I have chosen to not work on healing our relationship. It only made sense that I confront my past and let him know that the hurt he caused me has been forgiven. I so badly pray that he has asked for forgiveness and learned to forgive himself. I will spare you the details, but I will leave you with the outcome.

I confronted him and since that day I have not heard from him again besides one remark back that he suggests I seek counseling. Don't worry, dad. I have already done this. Maybe the restoration between the two of us won't happen on this side of earth, but I am hopeful that the way I have seen Jesus restore my soul will be the same thing that happens for my own father.

1. *Have you ever felt like you have some unresolved issues you need to address but despise confrontation?*

2. *Does the person who hurt you even know how badly wounded you are today?*

3. *Is it necessary to have those hard conversations with people in order for you to heal completely?*

4. *Does the idea of confronting someone that hurt you scare you more because restoration might happen or you are worried about their response?*

Chapter 16

Be Watchful

This world can be cold and bitter. The darkness that surrounds our everyday life can sometimes feel like too much. For some they never sense darkness and cannot even detect when it is around. Others of us know it is there and can't seem to get it to go away. All of us keep on trucking through life asking why so much bad could happen in our own little world or why we struggle with fear, doubt, shame, insecurities, and comparison. There is an answer to this. It is not an answer that a lot of people like to discuss. It seems more popular to talk about Jesus than it does to talk about Satan. The truth is that Satan is just as real as Jesus. If we don't wake up and begin to understand who he is and how powerful he is, we will never know when or how to fight off this thing called spiritual warfare.

As much as I love talking about Jesus you would think bringing up the bad guy in the story would be easy to mention, too. The reality is that he is much harder to bring up for a couple of different reasons. That conversation is not a happy, joyful one. It is a hard and deep conversation. It can sometimes creep people out or make them think I am crazy for believing in a guy that holds a pitch fork. But the truth of what the Bible has to say about who Satan is, is a truth we all need to understand. He is in the business of making all of our lives here on earth very difficult. He is trying to destroy our relationships, our family unit, our community. He is trying to tear you down individually. But you can never ever lose hope, and you must always remember that Jesus is so much more!

Talking about how you can be loved unconditionally even though you know you have sinned, understanding that you can live in complete freedom and no longer have to be enslaved to sin or the guilt and shame of sin is the most freeing concept to grasp. And the mere fact that Jesus offers you a free gift of salvation and you don't have to do anything to receive his love completely gets me excited to share with others.

I have noticed that when I do get bold enough to talk about the consequences of sin or the fact that there is this other character that will come into your life to steal, kill, and destroy it makes people very uncomfortable. There are a handful of topics people say you should never talk about in a group setting. Religion, politics, money and sex. It makes people uncomfortable. There are differences of opinions. But I am at a point in my walk with the Lord that I can't stay quiet about his love for others. I cannot possibly know this truth, and be walking in this freedom, and keep it all to myself. I want to shout it from the rooftop that Jesus Christ saved my life. He is my all in all. He is everything I was missing. He fills my cup. He comforts my soul. He brings me peace. He steadies my heart. He carries my burdens. He holds my hand.

I also have learned to **"be alert and of sober mind. Your enemy the devil prowls around like a roaring lion looking for someone to devour." 1 Peter 5:8** I recognize the other character in the story. He can so quickly become immersed in my daily life. If I am not carefully paying attention of his whereabouts, he will be there. This character can deceitfully find his way into my relationships and into my mind. He knows my weaknesses and knows where to come after me. He knows where I struggle and always goes straight for the kill. His purpose is to bring me down so that I may live under his authority believing all of the lies he tells me. It even says in **Ephesians 6:12 "For our struggle is not against flesh and blood, but against the rulers, against the authorities, against the powers of this dark world and against the spiritual forces of evil in the heavenly realms."**

I don't tell you about this to scare you. I tell you about this devil because he is alive and working fervently to take you down, too. I do not want to keep hearing about more broken marriages, friendships that are hurting, insecurities that we are believing about ourselves, and fear that we are choosing to live in, all because we are allowing Satan to rob us of the joy that Jesus offers. We are in this battle of life together. We Christians have to stick together and be able to call out this darkness. Bind up this evil one, and do not allow him into our own lives and the lives of those that we love. Remember in **Romans 12:2** where it says**, "Do not conform to the pattern of this world, but be transformed by the renewing of your mind. Then you will be able to test and approve what God's will is-his good, pleasing and perfect will.**

It is up to you, fellow sister, to let your light shine for all to see. Fight off the evil one, and do not believe the lies you hear him say to you every single day. Anytime you hear you aren't pretty enough, you aren't a good mom, your husband would be happier with another woman, well, then you aren't able to impact others … you need to look yourself in the mirror and say the truth of what the Bible says about you. You are fearfully and wonderfully made. God made you in his image. Be watchful and aware of who you chose to believe daily. Remind yourself of the gospel daily. Jesus came to rescue you. To call you home. To free you from living in the dark. He came to bring you life and life to the fullest. Trust him. Abide in him. Spend time with him. And do not let Satan get a hold of your life and tear you down. You are far more precious to the creator who created you.

1. *Why let Satan win?*

2. *Who will you believe and trust?*

3. *What lies do you hear over and over that you need to break with the enemy? (Some examples: I am fat, I am not worthy)*

4. *What would you like to tell Satan?*

Chapter 17

I Just Bought a Bleacher Seat

As I approach celebrating my 39th birthday this coming year, I cannot help but recognize the reality that is staring me in the face. I know age is just a number, but it is this year that I am physically noticing some changes in me. Changes that aren't necessarily bad, but changes that are obvious to admit that I might just be coming into a new decade with different types of aches, wrinkles, and interests.

I remember the nights when going out on the town sounded like a blast. I could not wait to throw on a new cute outfit and check out the newest restaurant or bar. It wasn't long ago that I could sit in my bed to read a book without the words ever seeming small or fuzzy. I recently purchased my first set of readers, and I feel pretty stinkin' cute wearing them. I finally have acquired a taste for wine and coffee- two drinks I thought only "old" people drank. I understand and appreciate the use of sunscreen. My idea of an awesome date night now consists of sitting on my porch snuggled next to my husband while we dream about growing old together and where we want to retire. Having a clean house actually matters to me as before I could have cared less. I recently had to color my grey hairs for the first time in my life. At the carpool line, I have noticed that I am no longer the young mom on campus. There are women there much younger than me. And what really has me reeling is the fact that this week I purchased my very first bleacher seat. I finally gave in after being tired of sitting on a hard bleacher while my back ached and my butt hurt.

Even with all of these aging signs, I still have never been able to admit that I might be growing up. I won't ever say I am growing old because I really believe age is just a number. I absolutely love the stage of life I am in right now. I know that is only because of my relationship with Christ. From an insecure doubtful young woman, to a mature and confident woman of God. I am embracing all that life has to offer and because of that I see God continuing to refine me. And when I read **2 Corinthians 4:16, "So we do not lose heart. Though our outer self is wasting away, our inner self is being renewed day by day."** I know God isn't finished with me, yet.

I imagine you are in a season of noticing changes of your own. Changes that may be a bit uncomfortable, unsettling, and even unnerving. Try to remember **Psalm 92:12–15, "The righteous will flourish like a palm tree, they will grow like a cedar of Lebanon; planted in the**

house of the Lord, they will flourish in the courts of our God. They will still bear fruit in old age, they will stay fresh and green, proclaiming, "The Lord is upright; he is my Rock, and there is no wickedness in him." As women of God, regardless of age, we can still bear fruit. Did you notice that the trees mentioned, the palm and the cedar, are known for vitality in old age? It's the whole idea of being "planted at the house of God"—faithfulness through the years. Keep in mind that the longer we decide to walk with God, the stronger our testimony will be.

So, here is some advice from your wise and aging friend: stop worrying about the minor changes to your body and your life. Be intimate with God, in sweet communion with him throughout your years to come. You will long to hear the sounds of the trumpet when it comes! And such a sound is coming!

1. *What physical changes are you noticing about yourself as you get older?*

2. *What spiritual changes are you noticing about yourself as you get older?*

3. *Are you more concerned with your appearance or your heart as you find out more about who God made you to be?*

4. *What are some changes in your life you would like to work on as you go into this next year of your life?*

Chapter 18

To My Inlaws

Oh, what I would do to have one day. Just one day with both of you here with our family. There are so many things I would want to share with you, and I often times think about how proud you would be of the life your son and I have built together. I wish so badly that you could know each one of your grandchildren. They are all amazing in so many different ways. I see many unique qualities in them that remind me of each of you from time to time. I find myself in tears during monumental moments that I miss not having you here to be a part of. I wonder how you would interact with them and what kind of role you would take in each of their lives. I am certain they would be given way too many gifts from you and that would probably be a discussion we would have to get on the same page about. But I know good and well that you would love each of them so deeply ... the same kind of unconditional love that you had for each other. I know without a shadow of a doubt that you would have loved them just as much as you so graciously loved me. You would be beaming with pride with every activity you could come and watch. You would laugh at their annoyances and take them from me to give me breaks and help me stay sane. You would show up for their activities and bend over backwards to be present in their lives. I also believe you both would be their biggest fans. Just like you were to your son and to me.

As much as I want you to know your grandkids and see all that the Lord has blessed your son and I with, what I desire even more is for you to know and see what an incredible man you raised. He is so much more than just a tall, dark, and handsome man. You both left this earth too early to see the fruits of your labor. You worked hard to raise your children and provide for them a loving and safe place to live. I want you to know that your work paid off tenfold. This man that you raised has experienced more heartache than most humans will ever encounter during a lifetime yet he has handled it with such grace. He has learned to be an overcomer and to look at the glass half full. He has identified who he is in Christ and how abundantly blessed he is for the life he has been given. He is a hard working man with a never give up kind of attitude. He is loud and funny. His kindness radiates onto others he is around. He is accepting of others regardless of their pitfalls. He always finds the best in people and never gives up on the ones he loves. I can think of many reasons he could hold grudges towards me but instead he has repeatedly shown me unconditional love. I love that he learned how to give because you both so willingly loved him that same way. He is more than I could have ever dreamed of and I oftentimes sit in wonder as to how I got so lucky to have him as my life partner. He literally is everything I could have ever dreamed of.

Lastly, I just want to thank you. You came into my life at a time when I needed it most. You gave me a visual picture that mirrors just how David felt about God's strength in **Psalms 59:16, "But I will sing of your strength, in the morning I will sing of your love; for you are my fortress, my refuge in times of trouble."** I needed to see a couple that would fight for each other. A couple that would never give up on each other even when the tough got tougher. You demonstrated such humility as your walls came crashing down around you and never raged with anger or resentment. Instead you boasted about the love you had for your family and how proud you were of each of your kids. You desperately wanted to live to meet your grandkids. I can vividly remember holding your hands at the last stages of both of your lives and talking about how badly you wanted to be able to see your grandkids. You have had a profound impact on the shaping of my life, and I am grateful for the short time I had on this earth with you both.

I promise to take care of your son for the rest of my life. We are committed to loving God first, and I know that with Jesus as our cornerstone we will be able to battle anything that gets thrown our way. I love you dearly and miss you always.

1. So ... inlaws ... I know they can be hairy relationships. How are your inlaws? Hard? Helpful? Annoying? Loving?

2. Are there ways you can better communicate with them of your needs so they can better serve you and you be less bitter towards them?

3. Have you ever sat and thought about what life would look like when they leave this earth? I encourage you to make the best of the time you do have with them.

4. Relationships are hard. I get it. But what could you do to help strengthen your relationship and involvement with your inlaws? Live with no regrets.

Chapter 19

Dry Bones Come Alive

I have been one hundred percent transparent to you throughout this story. And I won't stop here and tell you it is all roses once you are all in with Jesus. There will still be struggles and storms. You will crave time with him and then go through seasons when there seems like not one spare minute is available to spend with him. You will find that the one thing you need the most is time with Jesus, yet it's the first thing you give up. At least that seems to be the case for me. I can get going pretty smoothly in life and not make him a priority. The minute I do that my whole life starts to suffer. I am talking relationships crumble, impatience comes to an all-time high, I doubt myself, and start living with the old insecurities that I let rule my life for so long. And it happens quickly. So let this be a charge … a warning to you. Do not beat yourself up when you realize you have allowed yourself to slip away from him. Just wake up, repent, and ask him to grace you with his presence.

I recently went through a season without making him a priority and here was the prayer I cried out to him:

Father,

Forgive me for walking away from you and not depending on you for my every need. I finally understand what happens when we neglect you and try to think we can do life on our own. Please know that I never stopped thinking about you. I simply just didn't make you a priority and it shows. My heart is heavy. My eyes are weepy. My soul is longing to feel close to you again. There is no excuse and I find myself wondering why I could so easily let go of the one relationship that I know matters the most. It is so true that you are more than just our God. You are the epitome of relationship. It's crazy to think that you are always available and yet the first thing I push to the side. It reminds me of so many of my friends who would rather date the rebellious guy over the good guy. What is it about us that our needs and wants are so different and we usually go for the things we want and not need?

All I can say is that I am sorry and I miss you. Although I sing Dry Bones by Lauren Daigle every time it comes on the radio, today it meant something different to me. I think the words finally spoke to me, and I understand the magnitude of calling out to dry bones and asking them to come alive. So that is exactly what I am doing. Calling out for my dry bones to come alive. Breathe life back into me, Father. Breathe your Holy Spirit upon me, and help my dry bones come alive.

Amen

Guess what sisters … Jesus' arms are wide open and he never holds a grudge against our numerous times we fail him. Talk about undying love. Jesus is the real deal and choosing to pursue a life with him will only allow you to experience the real deal—**Galatians 5:22, "But the fruit of the Spirit is love, joy, peace, forbearance, kindness, goodness, faithfulness, gentleness and self control. Against such things there is no law."**

Chapter 20

Write Your Story

Romans 5:

"Therefore, since we have been justified through faith, we have peace with God through our Lord Jesus Christ, through whom we have gained access by faith into this grace in which we now stand. And we boast in the hope of the glory of God. Not only so, but we also glory in our sufferings, because we know that suffering produces perseverance; perseverance, character; and character, hope. And hope does not put us to shame, because God's love has been poured out into our hearts through the Holy Spirit, who has been given to us. You see, at just the right time, when we were still powerless, Christ died for the ungodly. Very rarely will anyone die for a righteous person, though for a good person someone might possibly dare to die. But God demonstrates his own love for us in this: **While we were still sinners, Christ died for us. Since we have now been justified by his blood, how much more shall we be saved from God's wrath through him! For if, while we were God's enemies, we were reconciled to him through the death of his Son, how much more, having been reconciled, shall we be saved through his life! Not only is this so, but we also boast in God through our Lord Jesus Christ, through whom we have now received reconciliation."**

I absolutely love the song "Good Good Father" by Chris Tomlin. "You tell me that you are pleased and I'm never alone... Many searching for answers far and wide...Peace so unexplainable I can hardly speak...I am loved by you. You are a good good Father." Every time I hear this song I cannot help but think about how my eternal Father has delivered me from a horrific past that is so hard to admit I even endured. A past that I lived with for many years hiding in shame, embarrassment, disgust, and disappointment. All along this good Father was and is still pleased with me. He has never left my side. I spent years searching far and wide, wrecking a lot of relationships along the way, and pretending I had it all together. There was no peace in my life. No joy to share and no love that I could give to others because I didn't even love myself. What a miraculous story of redemption!

I spent the last two years writing out my story from start to finish. It was hard. Lots of tears and emotions as I relived what I have been through. Also tears of joy as I saw first hand how God has rescued me and set me free to fly into a new beginning with a much bigger purpose than I ever would have imagined. Writing out my story brought more healing to my heart and let me sit in a place with Jesus truly feeling undeniably loved by him and knowing his call on my life.

In writing and now sharing my story with you, I hope it encourages you to self-reflect on your own life. Let me tell you ... facing the past was one of the most nerve racking things I have ever done. It was also one of the most exhilarating things I have ever done. Two years of prepping my heart and my emotions. Two years of figuring out how I can relay the message of just how great God is. Two years of intimacy with my maker as we sat together and sorted through what to share and how to bring him all the glory. God was with me every step of the way. He made it clear that my new purpose is to live out **Matthew 28:19 "Therefore go and make disciples of all nations, baptizing them in the name of the Father, Son and Holy Spirit."** I have been redeemed. Now my purpose is helping other women break every chain in the name of Jesus. There is power in his name, and there is freedom that he wants for each and every one of you.

Maybe you haven't seen redemption or experienced freedom in Christ. Maybe you still wonder how to get there with him. Maybe you are too scared to lay it all down at the cross and let go of the control. Maybe you don't know how to find Jesus and really know he is actually there. Here is what I can encourage you with today: Jesus is already with you right this very minute. He is madly in love with you and proud of how he made you. He has loved you with an everlasting love- *everlasting*- that means past, present and future! Jesus desires intimacy with you. That is what you were created for. To have an intimate and deep relationship with a good Father. All you have to do is seek him, turn to him, invite him into your life, hand over your sin, and ask him to lead the way. Go to him with your prayers, thank him for your praises, ask him to breath new life into your world.

Let this be a charge to write out your own story. Allow your heart to go to all of those dark places that you have been hiding or hurt for so long. Ask him to be with you as you recall your past or figure out your present. Ask him to show you his presence throughout your story. As you write and freely share your story you will be amazed to see that even in the midst of a lot of junk he has always been a part of the story. In fact, he hasn't just been a part of the story; he is the author still writing your story. Let him continue to write the greatest love story you will ever read. A love story of how he pursued you from beginning to end. How he never left your side and how he is celebrating victory since you have freely given your life over to him. You will experience Unexplainable Freedom and become the next Forgiven Sinner-just like me.

Printed in the United States
By Bookmasters